3 Minute Prayers

kevin mayhew

kevin
mayhew

First published in Great Britain in 2020 by Kevin Mayhew Ltd
Buxhall, Stowmarket, Suffolk IP14 3BW
Tel: +44 (0) 1449 737978 Fax: +44 (0) 1449 737834
E-mail: info@kevinmayhew.com

www.kevinmayhew.com

9 8 7 6 5 4 3 2 1 0

ISBN 978 1 83858 054 4
Catalogue No. 1501644

Cover design by Rob Mortonson
© Image used under licence from Shutterstock Inc.
Typeset by Rob Mortonson

Printed and bound in Great Britain

CONTENTS

PRAYERS FOR EVERYDAY MILITARY LIFE

Living out my faith at work

Dealing with change

For God's strength

PRAYERS FOR DEPLOYMENTS

PRAYERS THAT COUNT THE COST OF MILITARY LIFE

SAYING GRACE

A PRAYER ABOUT LEAVING THE MILITARY

PRAYERS FROM THE PAST

ABOUT THE CONTRIBUTORS

Writing prayers for the military is a specialist skill; it requires a deep understanding of how the military think, speak and what they want to pray about. This is too big a job for one person, as all three services (despite all being Armed Forces) think, speak and act differently, meaning that the issues for the Army are different from those of the Navy or the RAF.

Writing this book has therefore required a team approach. This team has been led by **Liesel Parkinson**. Liesel works as the Prayer Director for the Armed Forces Christian Union. She has written two other books designed especially with the military community in mind, and is currently working with others to provide a specifically Christian response to combat trauma and PTSD. As part of her job she spends hours praying with and for people within the military community from all three services. Many of the prayers in this book are the result of those conversations, prayers and over 25 years of marriage to a soldier!

Alex Barker joined the RAF in 2016 as a pilot and was streamed to fly multi-engine aircraft. His faith and trust in God have helped him through his flying training and the challenges of military life. He is passionate about sharing his faith with friends and colleagues and believes prayer is essential to service life.

A former professional Alpine Ski Teacher and Yacht Skipper, Padre **Geoff Berry** is now in his happy place living out of a bag on Ops or Ex, or riding his large motorbike. A life spent working out of doors has left Geoff with a profound respect for nature and the God who created it all. Nearly a decade working with soldiers has left him more reliant on prayer than ever.

Corporal **Elizabeth Driver**, serving in the Royal Air Force, is a Trustee for the Armed Forces Christian Union and a committee member of the Defence Christian Network. She found comfort in prayer whilst serving an operational tour in Afghanistan. As British female number one in Natural Luge, she is grateful that God is with her down the track, and in fact at all times!

Andy Earl was a police officer specialising in public order, before being ordained in the Church of England. He joined the Army in 2008 as a Padre and has served with various units, including the Airborne Engineers, Royal Irish, Harrogate AFC. He has deployed to Afghanistan, Cyprus, Mali and South Sudan.

James Francis is a Naval Chaplain based at the Armed Forces Chaplaincy Centre, part of the Defence Academy, where he helps with the formation and through-life training of military chaplains and other service personnel across all three services. Before becoming a priest he worked with rough sleepers in London.

Cole Maynard came to faith in the RAF and began his Baptist ministry in 1988, serving for 21 years as a Baptist Army Chaplain: with tours in Northern Ireland (2), Iraq (2), Afghanistan (2) and Africa (UN), retiring as Deputy Assistant Chaplain General. He is now Senior Minister at Colchester Baptist Church.

Charlotte Milne is a British Army wife, Royal Navy veteran and sister of a Royal Marine. Much of her life has therefore been heavily influenced by the Armed Forces and contributing to these prayers was an enjoyable way to reflect on these experiences.

Juliette Stokes is the Prayer Coordinator for the Armed Forces Christian Union, and married to Carl, an Army Padre. She has a real heart for praying for and supporting serving personnel and arranges for many of them to be prayed for regularly by AFCU's Prayer Support Teams. She has supported her husband in ministry for 25 years and in his military chaplaincy for the last 8 years.

Robert Whitethread is currently exploring his vocation after serving 24 years in the Band of The Scots Guards. During that time he travelled extensively with the band, and other members of the Armed Services, experiencing many of the high and lows of service life. Throughout this service his Christian faith sustained, supported, and challenged him, giving him many of the tools required to hold a long career in the Army, prayer being one of the most important of these. Robert is married to Libby, and enjoys a new life walking, cooking, and playing the recorder.

INTRODUCTION

This is a book for those serving in HM Armed Forces to use as a way into their own prayers, or to use when the well seems dry and they don't know how to pray. It has been written equally for those serving in the Navy, the Army and the Air Force and recognises the differences between them. A well-known analogy likens the different branches of the military to popular sports. The Royal Navy is like the crew that powers a modern streamlined rowing boat, pitting its collective skill with speed and determination in an international boat race. The Army is completely different; it is more like a team of rugby players, playing a fast and occasionally aggressive contact sport with a common goal but individual responsibility. Rugby players and the sport itself are more widely known about than rowing by the general public. This is true of the Army also, where everyone thinks they know what soldiers do and how they think and act. The RAF can be likened to

Formula One Motor Racing. Here, the real star of the show is the racing car and the driver of the car tends to get the attention and the glory, although everyone knows the team can affect whether they win or lose the race. When one thinks of the RAF, one thinks of the big, beautiful machines and the pilots who fly them, but there is a whole team of other people who are equally important to the functioning of the organisation.

Each branch of the military functions very differently to the others and has its own language and customs. However, there is common ground too. This book of prayers for the Armed Forces seeks to celebrate those differences while focusing on what unites them. Together, they seek to serve the nation of Great Britain by providing (if necessary) the ultimate force to safeguard her people and assets, giving their lives in this service if demanded. Serving in the Armed Forces is a noble and honourable calling but it can also be a hard one, creating tension and internal conflict for individuals, causing them to face up to the reality and cruelty of war and human mortality. It can put huge strain on families who spend long periods of time apart and face frequent moves and changes as those serving are deployed to wherever they are most needed.

The topics inside this small volume seek to reflect some of that diversity in military life. There are prayers dealing with the normal jogging; the daily grind of everyday life ashore/ in barracks and on the station. There are prayers dealing with deployment, postings and change. Then there are the prayers of lament. The prayers when the soul is distraught with the horror and reality of suffering and cruelty. These prayers are raw and broken. They do not attempt to speak platitudes, but wrestle with the big questions: Where is God in this? How can a loving God allow this? They can be uncomfortable to read, but rightly are included as prayers of lament to a loving God.

A Bible verse has been suggested to go alongside and to provide a context for each of the prayers, and to give those praying another platform from which to springboard their own heart's cries. A few historical prayers have also been included at the back, along with a service specific 'grace'.

3 Minute Prayers FOR THE ARMED FORCES

PRAYERS FOR EVERYDAY MILITARY LIFE

3 Minute Prayers FOR THE ARMED FORCES

LIVING OUT MY FAITH AT WORK

1

BLOCK LIFE

My people will live in peaceful dwelling-places, in secure homes, in undisturbed places of rest.

Isaiah 32:18

Lord,
I moved into my new room.
There are many like it but this one is mine.
I've made it my home,
a few personal touches.
There are always people around;
day and night.
It can be like living with my friends;
a non-stop party.
However, it can be like living in a zoo,
neighbours are loud, messy
and some of them a little smelly.
I feel caged, like I'm always being watched;
like I never get to relax.

Block inspections,
middle of the night fire alarms,
no hot water
and power cuts
all contribute to the daily life
of my military family.

Thank you that I am in your family,
that you know what I need,
you always provide
and because you are with me,
even on the tough days
I am never really alone.

Amen.

2

BUDDY-BUDDY SYSTEM

Always be prepared to give an answer to everyone who asks you to give the reason for the hope that you have. But do this with gentleness and respect.

1 Peter 3:15b

Lord,
being in the military means
I can make good friends.
Mates who are like family;
closer, sometimes.
And I am really blessed
by the guys and girls
you've put around me this time.
Thank you.
In the military we look out for our mates.
And I am bothered that they don't know you.

They think Jesus is just a swear word
and all priests are paedophiles.

Father,
I want them to see you.
To know you love them.
Made them.
Have a good plan for them.
I want them to see Jesus as the one who
died for them.
Welcomes them.
I mess up so often trying to tell them.
I speak when I should listen
and am silent when I really should tell them
about you.
Please use me.
Give me the right words at the right time.
So that they will see you are the one they've
been searching for
even though they didn't know it.

Amen.

CHAIN OF COMMAND

Don't let anyone look down on you because you are young, but set an example for the believers in speech, in conduct, in love, in faith and in purity.

1 Timothy 4:12

Lord,
I am proudly part of the military organisation,
with a hierarchical structure rooted deep in its core.
Sometimes I am grateful for the security this brings,
and sometimes it's a challenge.
People with their given authority making decisions,
sometimes their commands are confusing and hard to comprehend
but I have learnt to trust and follow them.

I am thankful that you are the King of kings
and the Lord Most High,
you only want to bless me and not to harm me
and no matter the orders from my chain
of command,
your plan for me will be fulfilled,
all in your time.

Amen.

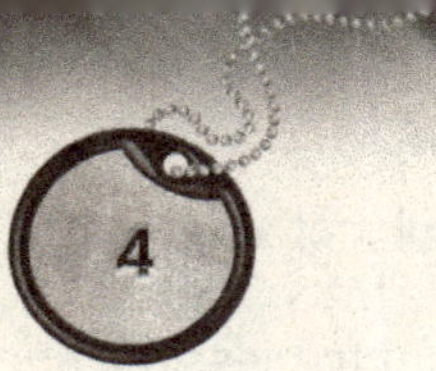

FINDING GOD IN THE MUNDANE

I will extol the Lord at all times;
his praise will always be on my lips.

Psalm 34:1

Dear Lord,
every day is the same.
The cleaning, preparing kit, carrying out duties.
How it wears me down in its relentlessness.
It doesn't feel like achieving.
How is this fruitful for your kingdom?
Or saving a nation?

You are here though.
I know that, Lord.
Help me to feel your presence.

Remind me that productivity isn't the most important thing.

Help me to incorporate praise into these boring tasks.
Keep my mind active and focused on you.

Amen.

ID

And we know that in all things God works for the good of those who love him, who have been called according to his purpose.

Romans 8:28

Father God,
who am I, when my name isn't preceded
by a rank?
In places where people don't salute me
at the gate.
Is my Christian name irrelevant?

It's easy, uniform requires no thought.
Even my civilian attire reflects my role.
My language and humour are heavily influenced
by the MOD now.
Is my character as well?

I know I am yours, Lord.
Does it show to those I meet?
Or am I institutionalised beyond recognition?
Just a Service number now . . .

I treasure this calling you have given me.
Please protect me from being overwhelmed
by the culture.
Help me to be true to who I am in you,
and grow in your likeness every day.

Amen.

6

JOBSWORTH

It may be that the Lord will look upon my misery and restore to me his covenant blessing instead of his curse today.

2 Samuel 16:12

Lord, help me today.
I'm gritting my teeth in frustration and angst.
We've been through the issue.
Again.
The answer the same,
'Can't change it.'
'This is the way it has to be done.'
I'm fighting inside against the irrationality of the position.
The way it makes no sense.
Defies logic. Costs more in time and energy.
I'm struggling with the attitude,
'Suck it up, Buttercup.'

I long to speak to someone who is not only
in charge
but can change the bureaucracy of the system.
Who sees this not as a problem or an issue,
with a cookie-cutter/one size fits all answer,
but as an opportunity to fine-tune the machine.
Becoming a better and more efficient people-
focused organisation.

I long for my voice to be heard.
Perhaps though,
you are teaching me patience, Lord.
Along with humility.
I know you want me to trust you and your ways
more fully.
Even when I can't understand.

I long to be a faster learner.
Help me to trust you in this too.
To praise you, despite the way things look.
To know that your plans and purposes for
my life will prevail,
no matter what the 'System' says.

Amen.

7

RATION PACK

How sweet are your words to my taste,
sweeter than honey to my mouth!

Psalm 119:103

Lord,
I've just got back from exercise.
Five days in the field eating 24-hour rations.
It was cold and wet
and I saved the bits I like the most as treats
to keep me going during a midnight stag:
smooth peanut butter, hard-boiled sweets,
the biscuits that come in the purple packets
and the Mexican chilli peanuts . . . Arriba!
I also managed to swap the false hope that is
the vegetarian all-day breakfast for my favourite,
menu 14 tomato pasta salad.

I was struck by the similarities between
    my approach to the Bible

and the way I pick through
    my packets.
There are passages I love to read
and those I find much harder.
I mean, I'm sure reading them is good for me
and feeds my spirit,
but I don't enjoy them very much.
Some of them are plain hard to swallow.
Pun intended!

So, Lord, I need your help.
Show me the verses you want me to read.
Send your Holy Spirit to open my eyes
to help me to understand what you are saying,
so that your word will be as sweet as honey.

Amen.

SOLDIER OF CHRIST

Join with me in suffering,
like a good soldier of Christ Jesus.
No one serving as a soldier gets
entangled in civilian affairs,
but rather tries to please his
commanding officer.

2 Timothy 2:3, 4

Lord God,
being in the military and being a civilian
are two completely different things.
Once I was a civvie, but now I am a soldier.
I follow orders, have to be on time.
Smartly dressed.
Fit.
I am disciplined. Organised even.
(Most of the time!)

But in my faith . . .

A soldier of Christ? Or a camp follower?
I know that there are times
when I've been a fan,
but not a real recruit with Jesus
as my commanding officer.
I've done things my way. Not his.
I've not sought to listen to his orders;
or put on my uniform, his 'spiritual armour'.
I wouldn't get away with this at work.
I realise I need to change.
Please forgive me, Father, and help me
start again.
To do things your way.
As a soldier in your army.
Following Jesus as my Captain and my King.

Amen.

9

WITNESS AT WORK

'In the same way, let your light shine before others, that they may see your good deeds and glorify your Father in heaven.'

Matthew 5:16

Ever-present Saviour,
you knew fun and laughter as well as
pain and sadness;
from turning water into wine
at the wedding at Cana,
to the death of your friend Lazarus,
and always you shone with
the radiant love of God.

Be with me, I pray, in all I do.
Pour out your Holy Spirit through me, Lord,
on the parade ground,
or in the NAAFI,

on the battlefield
or on a night out;
so that everyone I work with
will come to know your transforming love.
I pray this in the name of the Father,
    the Son, and the Holy Spirit.

Amen.

10

UP ABOVE THE CLOUDS

The Lord gives strength to his people;
the Lord blesses his people with peace.

Psalm 29:11

Father,
I've finished all the checks.
Everything is ticking along nicely.
We are a few hours into the flight
and in this brief moment,
I'm filled with your peace.
Keep my heart humble
and my faith strong.
So that when this moment of calm shatters,
I will know that your eternal peace remains.

Amen.

3 Minute Prayers FOR THE ARMED FORCES

DEALING WITH CHANGE

UNWANTED POSTINGS

Be strong and courageous.
Do not be afraid or terrified
because of them,
for the Lord your God goes with you;
he will never leave you nor forsake you.

Deuteronomy 31:6

Dear God,
I stand here before you,
scared and upset at this new posting
and chapter in my life.
You already know my fears and worries
about this,
yet I am going to tell you them anyway
because I know that you will listen
when I call out to you.

When I have finished,
fill my heart with peace and calm,
and then I pray, Lord,
that I will show the courage that your mother
    Mary had when she said 'yes'
to your calling to be mother to your Son,
my Saviour, Jesus Christ.
In his name I ask for this strength and peace.

Amen.

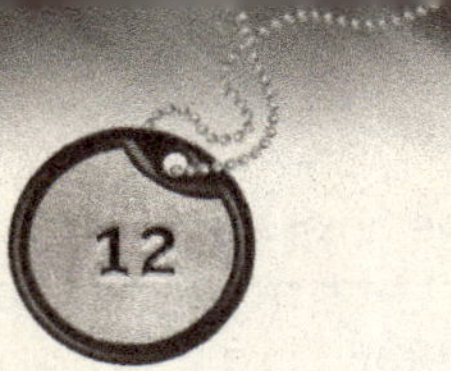

ALL CHANGE

There is a time for everything,
and a season for every activity
under the heavens.

Ecclesiastes 3:1

Lord Jesus,
you knew the stress and strain of change
all too well when you left the carpenter's shop
for the call to your earthly ministry.
Be with me at this time of upheaval and
uncertainty in my life.
I pray that you will give me the strength
and wisdom to be able to accept the change
in my life
with courage and maturity,
knowing that you are with me always.
I ask this in your name, loving Lord.

Amen.

FOR GOD'S STRENGTH

13

AIRSICK

'My Father, if it is possible,
may this cup be taken from me.
Yet not as I will, but as you will.'

Matthew 26:39b

Lord,
I thought I was over it,
this debilitating sense of inadequacy;
dizziness, nausea and an inability
    to finish the job.
At least here on the flight deck
I can see the horizon.
What's it like for those down back?
Please let this pass
and increase my tolerance,
so that I can feel normal.

Amen.

14

GREEN PT

With your help I can advance against a troop; with my God I can scale a wall.

Psalm 18:29

Father,
you and I both know that I am not as fit
    as I would like to be,
and my strength is failing
    as I march another mile.
I'm not sure I'm going to make it.
But I don't want to drop out
and have to do this again another day.
Give me strength to help me finish it.
I need mental resolve and physical energy.
Lots of it.
Oh . . .
and please could I have it now!!
Thank you.

Amen.

15

FEAR OF FAILURE

For the Spirit God gave us
does not make us timid,
but gives us power,
love and self-discipline.

2 Timothy 1:7

Loving God,
sometimes I spend so much energy
on trying to please the boss, my NCOs,
and my mates
that I forget that the only person
whose opinion really counts is you!
Help me to realise that when I feel a failure,
or feel that I have let my unit down,
you still love me no matter what.
That nothing I do or say
can take your unconditional love from me.

This wonderful truth streaks into my soul
like a brilliant ray of sunlight.
Thank you, Lord, for your unfailing
amazing love.
Help me to know you are near
when everyone around me
is telling me that I am not good enough.
I ask this in the name of him who died
that I might know your love forever,
Jesus Christ, my Saviour.

Amen.

FEAR OF FLYING

I said,
'Oh, that I had the wings of a dove!
I would fly away and be at rest.'

Psalm 55:6

Lord,
I am a leader and a warrior,
I am brave and I am strong.
I want to be an example to junior comrades,
I want to make my section proud.
I have a secret,
something I am ashamed to share
except with you, my Father.
You see, I'm afraid of flying.
I shudder from head to foot.
'Who will give me wings?' I ask.
'Wings like a dove.'

Please be with me when I fly,
to help me feel your presence and your peace,
so I can confidently fulfil my role
and be courageous.
To be the leader and the warrior
that you made me.

Amen.

17

SEASICK

**And my God will meet all your needs
according to the riches
of his glory in Christ Jesus.**

Philippians 4:19

Thank you for my health, Lord.
So often I take it for granted.
Today at sea I am reminded
how precious a gift it is!
Give those of us suffering, strength,
to conquer the tiredness and horrible feeling
of nausea.
A relentless hold on our bodies.

Give those who are well, strength.
Help them to be understanding and
compassionate.

Keep them in good health.
Give them the energy to cover our duties.
And when we dock, Lord,
help us to feel well when go ashore.
To feel stable when the movement stops.

Amen.

18

SLEEP DEPRIVED

Finally, be strong in the Lord and in his mighty power.

Ephesians 6:10

Dear Lord,
I am exhausted,
physically, mentally and spiritually.
The pace of work is relentless.
It doesn't feel safe.
My eyes no longer focus.
I fell asleep standing up today!
I long for rest.
Give me strength, Lord,
energy and a clear mind,
wisdom in my decisions,
help to achieve the task safely.

Amen.

3 Minute Prayers FOR THE ARMED FORCES

FOR GOD'S HELP

19

GIVING ORDERS

If any of you lacks wisdom,
you should ask God,
who gives generously to all
without finding fault,
and it will be given to you.

James 1:5

Lord,
at the start of this new day,
I'm thinking of all the challenges that lie ahead.
Decisions to make,
orders to give,
lives changed by my words.
I know that I need your wisdom,
the ability to understand,
to be insightful of the needs of the individual
as well as the mission.

Help me to make the right decisions.
To bring glory and honour to your name
in everything I do.
Help me to do my job well
for an audience of one.
You.
Not worrying about what others think,
or where my career is going.
But seeking to do things your way
for all that lies ahead.
In Jesus' name, I pray.

Amen.

20

HELP!

The Lord is my light and my salvation –
whom shall I fear?
The Lord is the stronghold of my life –
of whom shall I be afraid?

Psalm 27:1

Dear Lord,
help me to keep calm,
help me to breathe.
I am so afraid of getting it wrong.
But my panicked actions only serve to ensure
that is the case.

I am living my dream.
Yet I am so worried about having it taken away
that I am unable to enjoy it.

When I don't fully understand what they want,
give me the courage to ask for clarification.
Help me to remember that they are human too.

Help me to remember your promises
for my life.
Not to believe the lie that I am not enough.
Be with me as I strive to succeed.
Help me to praise you in my achievements.

Amen.

21

INSTRUMENT FLYING

**Though you have not seen him,
you love him; and even though
you do not see him now,
you believe in him and
are filled with an inexpressible
and glorious joy.**

1 Peter 1:8

Dear Lord,
we're in the cloud again.
It was a beautiful day back at Brize,
but now we have lost sight of the ground.
We've switched to instruments.
I trust the kit,
and the engineers who keep it serviceable.
I believe the aircraft will get me to my
destination.

It's easy to rely on what's in front of me,
but the disciples had their doubts
even though they had you to lead them.
Help me to trust you
    when I can't see the way ahead
and when I have to 'fly' by faith alone,
I trust you for a safe landing.

Amen.

22

MENTAL HEALTH

As for God, his way is perfect:
the Lord's word is flawless;
he shields all who take refuge in him.

2 Samuel 22:31

Father God,
I am finding it hard not feeling or acting like me,
I feel like I have lost control.
Lost my true self.
Controlled by emotions I wouldn't normally feel.
So strong that I am constantly on the brink of
losing control of myself.

On the surface I appear like I am coping.
Functioning relatively normally.
But there are subtle give-aways.

The reactions I take too far.
Behaving in a way that has no logic.
It is a downwards spiral of emotions.

But I know that you can help.
The eternal life won't have the troubles
    I face here.
Help me to see things through your eyes.
Keep me on course by the guidance of your
    loving hand.
Please show me who I can talk to
and where I can look to find your help.

Amen.

23

WHEN PRAYER WON'T COME

**He looked round at them all,
and then said to the man,
'Stretch out your hand.'
He did so, and his hand
was completely restored.**

Luke 6:10

Words don't come naturally to me, Lord.
I struggle to know the right thing to say.
Especially when I pray.
I get tied up inside.
What do you want to hear?
You are so great, so holy.
And there are so many big problems
in the world.
Are you really interested in my struggles
with my sergeant?

In where I'm posted next?
Today I read about Jesus healing a man
with a withered hand.
It was on the Sabbath. In the synagogue.
He was supposed to do nothing,
just sit and listen.
Maybe speak. But not make trouble, upsetting
the status quo.
But he refused. He cared too much for that
man with his duff hand.
It was only a hand. Just one.
But he noticed. He called him out. He cared.
He healed. No fuss. No questions.

So, Lord, I'm trusting you.
I know you're busy with important things.
But you also notice and care
about the little people.
Hear my prayers, even though I'm not very
good at praying them.

Amen.

24

A PRAYER BEFORE AN IMPORTANT BRIEFING

**'If you then, though you are evil,
know how to give good gifts
to your children,
how much more will your
Father in heaven give the Holy Spirit
to those who ask him!'**

Luke 11:13

Holy Spirit, come,
fill me,
guide me.
Let me know you are there.
Holy Spirit, come.

Amen.

EQUALITY AND DIVERSITY

DIVERSITY AND INCLUSION

'Blessed are those who hunger and thirst for righteousness, for they will be filled.'

Matthew 5:6

Father,
here I am, a woman in a man's world.
I know I belong here but others don't always see
it that way.
Help them to see past my physical appearance.
To respect my knowledge and experience.

Help me to know how to be a good role model.
To speak with your voice.
To earn their respect.
To actively demonstrate the strength
in diversity.

Help me to be an encouragement to others.
To enable 'the old boys' to journey through the changing dynamic.
To recognise when others are also struggling with acceptance,
and offer my support and friendship.

Keep me from being vulnerable.
Safe from unwelcome advances.
Accepting that sometimes I will be the only girl.
And trusting that you will use me in the place you have assigned me.

Amen.

26

FEMALE AND MILITARY

So God created mankind in his own image,
in the image of God he created them;
male and female he created them.

Genesis1:27

Lord,
I am grateful that I am me,
a female and a soldier, an airman or sailor.
Joining the British military gives me the
freedom to display
the specific qualities you gave to me
as a female:
nurturer, multi-tasker, defender.
Equal among my male peers,
but special in your eyes.
They'll never know the challenge of finding the
right colour tights

or turning up on a course and finding there is no
female accommodation.
But I'm glad I get to be 'one of the lads' whilst
still your precious daughter.
Please help me to use the power I have
to be the person you want me to be.
A princess and a warrior.

Amen.

27

THE ONLY ONE

Rejoice in the Lord always.
I will say it again: rejoice!

Philippians 4:4

Dear God,
it's so hard being the only one,
standing out for being different.
In my faith I am strong
but in other areas I am all alone.
The bittersweet runs ashore.
Grateful for the chance to explore,
but not fitting with the crowd.
Too senior to be their mate.
Too junior to be their mate.
The wrong branch for that crowd.
Attached, not part of the ship's company.
Surrounded by people but all alone.
Thank you for being there, Lord,
always listening to my prayers.

Amen.

28

BULLIED?

What, then, shall we say in response to these things? If God is for us, who can be against us?

Romans 8:31

O Lord,
please help me.
It's a weekday again!
Today I must face them.
I love my job, it's the persecution
    that weighs me down.
I was so excited about this assignment,
but now I dread getting to work.
Help me, Father, to love them as you do.
To avoid speaking from a place of hurt.
Help me to act how you did.
Rising above the pain when you walked the earth.
In your strength, not mine, Lord.

Amen.

29

VERBAL ATTACK

Though I walk in the midst of trouble, you preserve my life. You stretch out your hand against the anger of my foes; with your right hand you save me.

Psalm 138:7

Loving Lord Jesus,
I am having a rough time at work.
I am constantly being put under more pressure
than my colleagues,
and I feel picked on all the time.
I can't take the mickey-taking
or the vicious comments any more.

I need you to show me that you
are always with me, Lord.
You were bullied, Lord,
and I pray that I can be strong
when I'm facing those who are doing this.

I pray that you would give me courage
and grace to forgive them,
just as you forgave your persecutors.
I even ask that I show them love,
that they might come to know you, Lord.
I ask all this in your name,
Jesus Christ my Saviour.

Amen.

30

YES, I'M IN THE AIR FORCE. NO, I'M NOT A PILOT

Just as a body, though one, has many parts, but all its many parts form one body, so it is with Christ. For we were all baptised by one Spirit so as to form one body – whether Jews or Gentiles, slave or free – and we were all given the one Spirit to drink.

1 Corinthians 12:12, 13

Dear Lord,
I know pilots are important in the air force,
but some think they are on the
    same level as you!
We can't fly without them,
but we are the ones who get them in the air.

There's more of us than them
and I'm proud of what I do.
I know we are all on the same side;
all one team,
different roles but equally important.
However, you wouldn't know it from some
    people's perceptions.
I'm fed up with feeling second class
while pilots get all the cred.

You say blessed are the humble,
help me to remember that!
Let me do my job in a way that
    brings glory to your name,
whether or not it gets recognised or valued.
And, Lord, help me remember
next time I'm at church,
that this is all one team too;
and everyone is important.
Let me notice the ones who get overlooked,
and appreciate their service too.

Amen.

A FEW SERVICE-SPECIFIC PRAYERS

31

A 'NORMAL' DAY IN THE ARMY

Your love, Lord, reaches to the heavens,
your faithfulness to the skies.

Psalm 36:5

Lord,
it's been nine years since I joined
and the longer I stay in, the bigger the gap
between what I do now
and what I did then.
Tours in Afghan, Africa, Estonia
    and Cyprus.
More 'nights out of bed' than seems
    truly possible.
I've seen things,
been part of things; some good, some sad.
They've changed me.

Strengthened me.
Made me grow up.

My wider family and civvie friends
    ask me to tell them
what a 'normal' day looks like and I say,
    'It depends.'
On ops, there's a rhythm, a routine . . .
a cause.
I'm part of something bigger.
There is energy, adrenaline and mates.
At home that rhythm changes
and I put children to bed,
pay bills
and enjoy time away from pressure.

Throughout it all
your hand sustains me,
makes me who I am.
Gives me grace to do my job.
Gives me hope when things are hard.
Gives me strength to carry on.
Thank you.

Amen.

32

A PADRE'S PRAYER

We are therefore Christ's ambassadors, as though God were making his appeal through us. We implore you on Christ's behalf: be reconciled to God.

2 Corinthians 5:20

Lord,
if you had told me seven years ago
about the things I would be doing today
I would have scratched my head in wonder.
I have always felt in awe and marvelled
that you would call me to the ministry,
even if I often felt like a maverick
in my rural parish.

My delight in you has become more
pronounced
as I've made my home here among the military.
Turns out they like parish mavericks!

I'm thankful for the banter,
the acceptance of the padre as part of the unit,
the conversations which spring from
    that belonging,
the opportunities to answer the
    earnest questions
that spring from those conversations.
It is a privilege to answer the honest questions
which result from these discussions,
and to share the gospel with young people
who are aware of their mortality
and want honest answers.

I pray for your stamina today.
For the right words.
To know when to shut up.
Most of all for the humour which gets us all
    through the tough times.
I ask for the simple conversations today
which can turn to sharing the good news
    of Christ,
leading to repentance and changed lives
for your glory.

Amen.

33

AFLOAT ON THE OGGIN

(NAVY)

Have I not commanded you?
Be strong and courageous.
Do not be afraid; do not be discouraged,
for the Lord your God will be with you
wherever you go.

Joshua 1:9

Lord,
I'm joining my ship for the first time today.
I'm both excited and anxious.
It's not always easy to join a ship
    that is already at sea.
People are settled.
Established friendships.
Known routines.

Breaking in will be hard,
harder than if I'd been there from the start!
Thank you for your promise
to be with me
wherever I go.
Help me to be strong
and very courageous!

Amen.

34

'NOTHING SURVIVES CONTACT WITH THE ENEMY'

(RAF)

**'Your kingdom come, your will be done,
on earth as it is in heaven.'**

Matthew 6:10

Lord,
I'm sat here on the runway.
We were meant to be here 30 minutes ago.
Just to do that has been tough;
flight plans were delayed,
the aircraft had several snags,
and even getting out of the house this morning
was hard;
slowed by my dog who wanted to play.

As they say, 'Nothing survives contact with
the enemy.'

I'm looking ahead to take-off
and everything that could go wrong today.
What will the weather be like when we arrive?
Will the aircraft pick up more faults during
the flight?
Are we going to get back on time?
And who will look after the dog if I'm delayed?
So many questions that squeeze and
choke me.
Even though they say, 'Leave everything
outside the bubble'
it's not something I'm finding easy now.

Thank you, God, that I don't have to do it
on my own,
that you are sovereign.
You are the one truly in command,
despite all my efforts.
Despite the changes that will happen.
So, Lord . . .
I'm taking a deep breath, looking up and saying
whatever happens today, your will be done.
Your kingdom come.

Amen.

3 Minute Prayers FOR THE ARMED FORCES

PRAYERS FOR DEPLOYMENTS

35

ABOUT TO DEPLOY

Cast all your anxiety on him
because he cares for you.

1 Peter 5:7

Lord, the moment has finally come for us to go.
The preparations have gone on for so long
at times I thought this moment would
never come.
My heart is full of mixed emotions.
I want to get out there and get on with the task
in hand,
to be able to 'do my bit'
and feel like I am making a difference.
I want to hold up under pressure,
to do well and not make any mistakes or
look the fool.

Lord, I am buzzing with questions that
    I don't know the answers to.
I don't want to ask my mates and look like a
    worrier so I'm bringing them to you.
What will I really find when I get there?
How will I cope?
How easily will I be able to put my training into
    practice in real situations on the ground?
Lord, will people really have my back
    if it all goes wrong?
Will I get on with the team
    when we are living so closely for so long?
How will I cope without any real space to myself
    for months on end?

How will I cope with the teasing if I let on that I
    am a Christian and go the padre's services?
How can I be true to my faith and still be one of
    the lads?
How will I cope away from home
    for the first time?
And what will I be coming home to?
Will my partner still be waiting for me nine
    months down the line?

How can I stop my parents from
worrying about me?
How much communication will I have with them
while I am away?
Lord, I need your help, your strength,
your peace.
Please, Lord, I really need it now.

Amen.

36

BE STILL

**He says, 'Be still,
and know that I am God.'**

Psalm 46:10

In the raging waters of my life:
Be still and know.
In the pressure of commitments:
Be still and know.
In the uncertainty of the future:
Be still and know.
In the tumult of the meetings:
Be still and know.
In the stress of my marriage:
Be still and know.
Lord, help me to be still and know today that
you are God
and that I can find rest and trust in you.

Amen.

37

APART

Cast your cares on the Lord and he will sustain you; he will never let the righteous be shaken.

Psalm 55:22

Father,
this is too much!
I know I signed the dotted line,
I saluted and marched off the square,
    but I miss them!
I miss them terribly and just want to be there
    with them and not here in this place.
I know we call it service.
Separation with a purpose, for a noble cause,
fighting for those who can't, providing security,
    aid and hope – but what about my needs?
I too need family.
I need to hear their voice, their touch,
    their smell,

to be in their arms rather
    than just bearing them.
I am no rock and we know that 'no man is
    an island',
and yet here I am, isolated from those who mean
    the most to me
and a vast ocean separates them from this lonely
    isle called me.

And there is the fear:
the knowledge that people don't always
    come back.
That death can be the reward to pin
    on my chest
in this place of anguish and conflict.
That thought is too much to bear,
that I might never see those smiles again,
and hear the tinkle of their laughter,
the caress and warmth in their eyes.
God help me in this place!

Amen.

38

EVEN IN THAT PLACE . . .

When Jacob awoke from his sleep, he thought, 'Surely the Lord is in this place, and I was not aware of it.'

Genesis 28:16

Lord Jesus,
life has been so hard.
I have felt pressure from all sides.
Feeling alone.
Afraid.
Abandoned by you and away from my friends.
I have not had any say in where I wanted to go
or what I wanted to do.
Instead, the decisions have been made
    by others
and they are not the ones I would have made.

I've wondered why you have allowed this.
I've been hurt by your silence.
I've stopped trying to listen to you –
not wanting to hear your voice.
Then today I read this verse
about Jacob asleep in the desert.
Alone.
Afraid and running away.
Isolated and wounded,
victim of his own poor choices.
But you had not abandoned him,
in fact, you promised to be with him.
Even though he lied. Cheated. Stole
from his brother.
You were there. With him.
Even in that place.

Maybe today I'll allow myself to believe a little . . .
that you haven't given up on me.
That you love me.
Hear me.
And that you are here. Even in this place.
Even though I am not aware of it.
Yet.

Amen.

FIRST DEPLOYMENT

**So do not fear, for I am with you;
do not be dismayed, for I am your God.
I will strengthen you and help you;
I will uphold you with
my righteous right hand.**

Isaiah 41:10

Lord, I'm far from home.
My first deployment
and I'm thinking of all that lies ahead
and those I've left at home.
I'm excited to finally be here.
All that training can now be used.
I'm with my mates and the banter's great.
I get to save some money and see
a foreign country.

But I am also anxious . . .
Have I got what it takes?
Will my marriage survive?
Will my kid recognise me when I get back?
Where will you be in this place?
Strengthen me and help me.
Let me know your presence and your peace.

Amen.

40

FOR LOVED ONES BACK AT HOME

Your love, Lord, reaches to the heavens, your faithfulness to the skies.

Psalm 36:5

Father, please help!
PLEASE HELP!!
I don't know what to do
except
to cry out to you!
Knowing that you always hear me
when I pray.

I'm far from home today,
working hard at my job,
but I'm anxious about my family.
You know how upset my wife was
when we spoke last night.

The issues with the kids;
their health and that thing at school.
You know the car broke down
. . . again
and the washing machine jammed.
I'm not there to help.
Again.
And now she's not answering
and I don't know if she's coping and getting on
with it all
in her incredible way
(but feeling resentful to me, my job and
my absence),
or whether something is really wrong.

What do I do?
Please let her know that you are near to her,
surround her with awareness of your love
and presence.
Give her strength.
Give us time to talk this through.
Bless our marriage and our family life.
In Jesus' name.

Amen.

41

'HANDS TO ACTION STATIONS'

There is no fear in love.
But perfect love drives out fear,
because fear has to do with punishment.
The one who fears is
not made perfect in love.

1 John 4:18

Lord,
today we had the pipe,
'HANDS TO ACTION STATIONS,
HANDS TO ACTION STATIONS',
then straight away
the sea state changed
as we increased our readiness to take damage.
Water-tight hatches,
closed.
Ship's company,
split:

teams of fire-fighters; first-aiders;
stretcher-bearers; power re-routers and
damage control.
Ahead we could see some Fast Inshore
Attack Craft
coming our way.
Adrenaline pumped.
Tensión rose.
And around me the white faces of a
few young hands.
They had never gone to action for real before.

In the end,
a false alarm.
A show of strength.
Situation normal again.
I'm glad you're there, Lord,
no matter what happens,
promising that your perfect peace casts out
all fear.

Amen.

42

ON OPS

Whoever dwells in the shelter of the Most High will rest in the shadow of the Almighty.

Psalm 91:1

Strengthen me and sustain me
so I can do my duty by both those here
and those back home.
Chase away those dark thoughts
and give me courage to serve the right
and salute the noble cause I seek to live.

Help me be the better me.
Shape me in the gym of prayer
to better be like that great soldier, Jesus Christ,
who fought the darkest ever battle and cried:
'Not my will but yours!'
I want my will; I long for my way,

but know yours is never the highway,
but always the best.

Father, I need you to father me
and give me that strength of body,
    soul and spirit,
to be yours in this place,
for these people,
for this time.

Amen.

43

PAUSE BEFORE TAKE-OFF

(BASED ON THE HYMN, BE THOU MY VISION)

**My God is my rock, in whom I take refuge,
my shield and the horn of my salvation.
He is my stronghold,
my refuge and my saviour.**

2 Samuel 22:3a

Almighty God,
you are my battle shield,
sword for the fight.
You are my dignity
and you're my delight.
You are my shelter,
you are my strong tower.
Come raise me heavenward,
great power of my power.

Amen.

44

POST-DEPLOYMENT BLUES

The Lord himself goes before you
and will be with you;
he will never leave you
nor forsake you. Do not be afraid;
do not be discouraged.

Deuteronomy 31:8

Lord,
I'm now safely home from tour,
and did things I didn't know I could.
My role was important and
my orders were followed immediately.
I worked hard; I never stopped.
I had a purpose.

Now I'm home
and I have to queue in the supermarket for
things I need,

people shuffling aimlessly up and
    down the aisles,
just getting in my way.
Children screaming for no reason at all,
just adding to the noise,
and the party for my safe return seems
    so pointless
when compared to the reality of my tour.

I thank you that you're with me
and that you understand.
Through your strength I know this reality
will become my new normal.
Please show me the way to find peace.

Amen.

**PRAYERS THAT
COUNT THE COST
OF MILITARY SERVICE**

PRAYERS OF ANGUISH AND CONFUSION

45

DISASTER RELIEF

Do not be anxious about anything, but in every situation, by prayer and petition, with thanksgiving, present your requests to God. And the peace of God, which transcends all understanding, will guard your hearts and your minds in Christ Jesus.

Philippians 4:6, 7

God . . . WHY???
How could you have allowed this to happen?
If I'd landed here a month ago,
there would have been a vibrant community;
life to the full.
Now all I can see is death, illness,
    hunger, suffering.
The wind has levelled the houses.
The tide has swept away lives.

The last time I saw suffering like this was in
a war zone
I know that man can be cruel.
But surely not you?

I know that you are good.
I know that you are loving.
I cannot see the good in this,
but I trust you.
I have faith in you.
And I know that there is that other scene of
suffering:
you – nailed to a cross.
In my place.
And behind that, the empty tomb.
That is the only light in this dark place.

Amen.

46

STORM

I cry out to you, God, but you do not answer; I stand up, but you merely look at me. You turn on me ruthlessly; with the might of your hand you attack me. You snatch me up and drive me before the wind; you toss me about in the storm.

Job 30:20-22

Father,
how can this be happening?
How can I face yet more shit,
in this world that seems to offer little more than
frustration and pain?
Where are you in all this?
I believe,
at least I want to believe in you,
but the sheer depth of this shit storm
overwhelms me and the light goes out!

How can there be no light at the end of
my tunnel?
Why is my tunnel so long and so bloody dark?
Where are you, Father God?

People say that above the cloud, no matter
how thick, the sun always shines,
but I need more than that!
I need a crack in those clouds, a shaft of light
rather than just being shafted!
I believe . . . help me with my unbelief!
I cry: hear, hear my voice!
I implore, give me a break, an end,
a light to this darkness;
a sense that you are here in this cancerous,
steaming mire with me.
Hear me.
Help me.
Be with me.

Amen.

THE DARKNESS

'And surely I am with you always,
to the very end of the age.'

Matthew 28:20b

Father,
didn't your Son say, 'I will never leave you or
forsake you?'
So where is he now?
Here I am in this mess and pain,
and yet the Light of the World has gone out!
Or so it seems to me.
Darkness seems to be everywhere,
and you seem so very far away,
distant, uncaring, remote!
How can you make such promises,
and yet not be around to deliver when I need
you most?

I try and pray, but there seems to be concrete
between you and me;

like a bunker, but it's keeping you out and
the pain in!
Yet I know there is nowhere I can escape your
presence,
that you are everywhere,
even in this shit;
this existence that I currently call my life.
The pain is just too much – I can't seem
to cope.
Yet you did, Lord Jesus, with that cross
they nailed you to.
Your face, marred by blood and snot,
tears and sweat
as you tried to sort out our mess on this crappy
little planet.

Help me now!
Help me cope with my pain and the mare
that engulfs me.
Don't turn your face from me.
Don't hide your presence.
I feel so alone, but then feelings are
so unreliable,
so perhaps you are here, I just don't 'feel' it?

Was it you that nulled the pain for a while
the other day,
you who spoke through the smell of a flower
and the song of a bird?
Is that you? Trying to break into this bunker of
shit and despair?
I hope so.
Help me see; help me sense; help me find you.

Amen.

3 Minute Prayers FOR THE ARMED FORCES

THE REALITY OF DEATH AND DYING

48

BAD NEWS

**He will wipe every tear from their eyes.
There will be no more death or mourning
or crying or pain, for the old order
of things has passed away.**

Revelation 21:4

Weep? If I could but weep,
but moisture's too precious
and is spent by my pores in this heat!

Cry? If I could I would.
But my body, savaged by the sun,
has little water left to try.

Shout? If I could but be heard,
but deaf ears all around
seem to ignore the sound of my muted word.

It is here, in this hole of powerless frustration,
at the mercy of one's situation, that I struggle
to find help.

Darkness! It is all around, no light to be found;
the tunnel endless in its length; the silence
profound.

Where is the end?
To swim for the shore only to find
that the length you have swum
is the journey just begun.

Amen.

(Maysen Province, Iraq, 22nd May, 2003)

49

HOW AWKWARD

Even though I walk through the darkest valley, I will fear no evil, for you are with me; your rod and your staff, they comfort me.

Psalm 23:4

Lord,
I was struck on a recent visit to the theatre to
see Les Mis
(a show I had seen 20 years before
and a show my wife hadn't seen before),
how situations and experience
change our reality.
There is a memorable scene where
the hero returns,
following the battle to the bar of his youth.
All his friends are dead and reappear
to provide a ghostly chorus.

I was transported back to Afghanistan,
to the friends we said farewell to,
especially one chap who was leaving the base,
he on a foot patrol and me, mobile.
We agreed to take dinner later that day
as we were both due at Bastion.
As I arrived
MINIMISE was on
and I was called to the hospital.
A meeting in Bastion but not the one
we had hoped for.
I was able to pray with and for him
and so began his final journey
to his family and to life immortal.

In the theatre my tears flowed again,
as did the certainty
that what we are called to be matters.
Lord, you journey with us and you provide
    my constant hope and reassurance
that all will be well.
Thank you for your loving care.

Amen.

50

REMEMBRANCE SUNDAY

Praise be to the God and Father of our Lord Jesus Christ, the Father of compassion and the God of all comfort, who comforts us in all our troubles, so that we can comfort those in any trouble with the comfort we ourselves receive from God.

2 Corinthians 1:3, 4

Dear God,
be with our nation today.
Help me to find the words,
  to tell what it means to us.
The reason why my shoes are extra shiny today.
All the faces I see reflecting from their
  bulled surface.
The friends I so desperately miss.
Help me stand a little taller,

eyes focused on you and them at your side
in heaven.
Help me stand a little stiller,
knowing your peace in my troubled heart.
Let the silence speak respect into the hearts
of our nation.
Let the service be worth the sacrifice.
Help me remember who I am really fighting for.

Amen.

51

THE CORDS OF DEATH ENTANGLED ME

Where, O death, is your victory?
Where, O death, is your sting?

1 Corinthians 15:55

Lord,
I know I put on a good act.
Tough.
Confident.
I push myself to take risks.
Others think I am not afraid of anything.
The truth is there is a pool of fear buried deep inside.
So big I can hardly breathe.
I keep it down.
Stop it bubbling up.

Once I met a soldier during a frenetic tour who told me he was afraid.

He didn't look it.
Said he was afraid of lots of things:
missed opportunities,
letting people down,
people dying when he could have saved them.
But inside he had this peace.
Then I realised.
Even though he was afraid, he did not fear
death itself.
He knew for sure that you had a place for
him today,
tomorrow, or many years from now.
One day he would enter that door and
be with you.

Lord, give me this peace.
To know that my future is decided.
I too, want to be unafraid to die
so that I can truly live today.

Amen.

52

SUICIDE OF A MATE

The Lord is close to the broken-hearted and saves those who are crushed in spirit.

Psalm 34:18

Lord, I am so angry, how could this have
happened?
Why did you let it happen to him?
We sign up knowing that we may die in action,
but we don't sign up for this!
We don't plan for this.
It's such a waste, he had so much to live for.
He should be here, getting ready for a great
night out with his mates.
Why isn't he here!
Why didn't he talk to me? We were best mates.
Why didn't I see the signs? Why? Why? Why?

He was the life and soul of the party.
The one who always made a joke
to cheer you up.
How come he's the one in the coffin?
The one who couldn't go on?
The one who ended it all?
Where were you, God?
Where are you now?
I need to know that you are still in control,
I need to know that you were there with him
in his pain.
I can't cope with this alone, it's too raw,
it's too painful, it's too sad.

Jesus, I know you are Lord of all.
I know that you are still sovereign,
but this doesn't seem right, this is so unfair.
I know that you are crying with me
and that your heart is aching with pain like mine.
I know that you are grieving for his loss too.
Please come close, please give me the strength
to keep going . . .
to be there for his family.
Lord, I need your hope to fill me so that I can
bring your comfort to everyone else.
And Lord, I know that there are others.

Those overwhelmed by pain;
the grief and trauma of things they've seen and
done.
Lord, tune me in so that I can hear what isn't
being spoken aloud.
Let me hear those who are also in need.
Lord, please don't let this happen again.

Amen.

3 Minute Prayers FOR THE ARMED FORCES

SAYING GRACE

53

A NAVY GRACE

It is not unusual for junior ranks to be called to 'say Grace' before a formal meal. These graces are usually light-hearted and relevant to their military context and said in front of a primarily non-Christian audience. This naval grace, loosely following the pattern of the Lord's Prayer, is common of this genre. It is not intended to cause offence.

Our Father,
who art somewhere considerably drier than this,
hallowed be scran time.
Cheesy hammy eggy come.
Vegetable roulette be won.
In the galley as it is in heaven.
Give us today pusser's fresh scran.
And forgive us for double duffing,
as we forgive those who invented UHT milk.
Lead us not into the queue behind Royals,
and deliver us from limp veg.
For yours is the kingdom, the power
    and the glory.
Forever and ever.

Amen.

54

AN RAF GRACE

Bless us all in this family of light blue,
those from the past, the present and
brand new.
As we remember the days gone by
of time at home and in the sky.
Looking to the future as we dine,
we thank you for this evening's food and wine.
And when this meal is over,
the dessert the final course,
please be with us and protect us,
all the members of the Royal Air Force.

Amen.

55

AN ARMY GRACE

Dear Lord,
as we meet together in this Mess,
we ask you, Lord, our food to bless.
Be with each of us who gather here
who have travelled both from far and near
to raise a toast to the brave and bold
and hear of stories as yet untold.

Amen.

3 Minute Prayers FOR THE ARMED FORCES

A PRAYER ABOUT LEAVING THE MILITARY

56

SEVEN CLICKS TO FREEDOM

Trust in the Lord with all your heart and lean not on your own understanding; in all your ways submit to him, and he will make your paths straight.

Proverbs 3:5, 6

Lord,
I need your wisdom as I think about my life.
Should I continue to do this job
working in the Armed Forces,
or should I start again?
Something new.
Enter into the unknown.
Having joined up straight from school,
there are lots of things about life in civvie street
I don't know.
I've come to appreciate the regular pay cheque;
job security;

a ready-made community;
a home to live in wherever I move.
Even if those choices, made for me,
    frustrate me,
they provide a safety net for life.
In many ways, this job is more than what I do.
It's become who I am.

Can I leave it all behind
and start again?
And do something completely different
without the crutch of military life?
My fingers pause over the keyboard.
Seven clicks and I'm out.
But should I stay or should I go?
Lord, give me wisdom and peace
to know what your will for my life is.

Amen.

PRAYERS FROM THE PAST

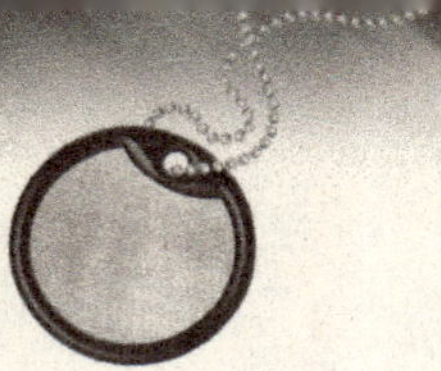

Before the Battle of Edgehill 1642

Prayer of Sir Jacob Astley

O Lord, thou knowest how busy I must be this day. If I forget thee, do not thou forget me.

Prayers of Ignatius of Loyola

Ignatius (1491–1556) was a soldier.
While wounded in battle, he encountered God
and devoted the rest of his life to following him.

Teach us, good Lord,
  to serve you as you deserve;
to give, and not to count the cost,
to fight and not to heed the wounds,
to toil and not to seek for rest,
to labour and not to ask for any reward,
except that of knowing that we do your will.
Amen.

Suscipe (Receive)

Take Lord, and receive all my liberty,
my memory, my understanding,
and my entire will,
all that I have and possess.
Thou hast given all to me.
To thee, O Lord, I return it.
All is thine,
dispose of it wholly according to thy will.
Give me thy love and thy grace,
for this is sufficient for me.

St Patrick's Breastplate

A shortened version of the famous prayer of Ireland's most favourite saint is included below. Legend has it that he prayed it faithfully during the dark days before he successfully converted the Irish king and his followers to Christianity. The breastplate is the ancient equivalent of body armour. (Circa 433)

I arise today
through a mighty strength,
the invocation of the Trinity,
through belief in the Threeness,
through confession of the Oneness
of the Creator of creation.

I arise today
through the strength of Christ's birth
    with his baptism,
through the strength of his crucifixion
    with his burial,
through the strength of his resurrection
    with his ascension,
through the strength of his descent for the
    judgement of doom.

I arise today, through
God's strength to pilot me,
God's might to uphold me,
God's wisdom to guide me,
God's eye to look before me,
God's ear to hear me,
God's word to speak for me,
God's hand to guard me,
God's shield to protect me,
God's host to save me
from snares of devils,
from temptation of vices,
from everyone who shall wish me ill,
afar and near.

Christ with me,
Christ before me,
Christ behind me,
Christ in me,
Christ beneath me,
Christ above me,
Christ on my right,
Christ on my left,
Christ when I lie down,
Christ when I sit down,
Christ when I arise,
Christ in the heart of every man
who thinks of me,
Christ in the mouth of everyone
who speaks of me,
Christ in every eye that sees me,
Christ in every ear that hears me.

Sarum Primer 1558

God be in my head and in my understanding;
God be in my eyes and in my looking;
God be in my mouth and in my speaking;
God be in my heart and in my thinking;
God be at my end and in my departing.

Sir Francis Drake

(circa 1540–1596)

O Lord God,
when you permit your servants
to attempt any great matter,
let us know that it is not the beginning,
but the continuing of the same to the end,
until it is thoroughly finished,
which yields the true glory,
through him who for the finishing of your work
laid down his life, our Redeemer, Jesus Christ.

Amen.

Based on Oliver Cromwell

(1599 – 1658)

Lord,
we have served our country
  faithfully in this operation,
honestly believing in the justice of our cause.
Do not let us be discouraged, but give us true
  thankfulness and humility,
so that we, who have ventured our lives for the
  freedom of our country,
may trust you for the freedom of our
  conscience,
and our government to maintain the freedom
  for which we fight.

Amen.

For your own reflections and prayers